Katherine A. Rayne's

LOST IN THOUGHTS

ADULT COLORING BOOK

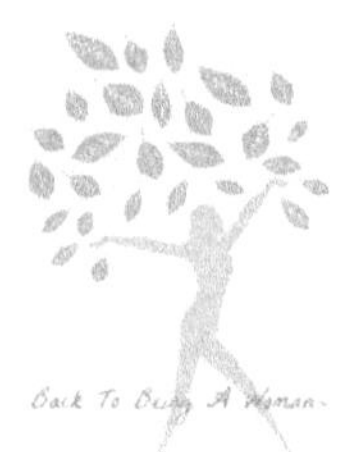

Published November, 2015

Designed by Katherine A. Rayne

Contact Email Address:

Katherine@KatherineARayne.com

Manufactured in the

United States of America

ISBN #978-0-9910552-6-5

This Book is Dedicated to

My Mom,

The Artist of my Heart

This Book

Belongs to:

____

Other Books by

Katherine A. Rayne

Back to Being a Woman

(Without Changing the Man)

There's a Light at the End of the Tunnel. You.

#Live Simply #Live Elegantly Your Life Journal

Introduction

Coloring is the perfect activity to help me get lost in my thoughts. It feels like a simple form of meditation to me. When I'm stressed, instead of pulling out my hair, I pull out my sketching pad. Drawing or coloring brings me back to earth and grounds me. I need something that rescues me from my busy life so that I can replenish and regroup in an easy and carefree way. The colors come to life as I come back to life.

Whether I color inside the lines or outside the lines, coloring allows me to weave pieces of my life onto the pages with colorful shades and tones. I use darker shades for darker thoughts and lighter shades for my lighter thoughts.

Coloring and bringing life to a blank page also lets me create something new. The choices of colors, designs and intensity are endless and mine to decide. I go to a better place when I'm drawing, even if it's just for 20 minutes. It's the perfect go-to when I'm brain dead after a long day or week.

Coloring is even better alongside my daughter. It becomes "together" time. We talk about simple things or just go quiet sitting side by side. When we're finished, no matter how the joint venture turned out, we always have something that we admire; each other.

I love all of the beautiful adult coloring books that I find in bookstores and online, but haven't bought one yet. When I browse through their pages, I become overwhelmed. I have a bad habit of starting projects and then not finishing them, and the coloring pages that I come across are all so articulate and detailed, I know I'll never finish one. I'd rather have a fun, relaxing 20 minute time-frame kind of page, not an hour and a half/oh-no-I'll-never-finish-this-it's-too-much! kind of a page. I'm trying to reduce my stress, which is the purpose and the reason for the adult coloring book popularity. So guess what I did. I created my own coloring book with much simpler illustrations so that it doesn't overwhelm me, and now I'm sharing it with you.

I took my coloring book a step further. We all wear crowns in life. Some of our crowns might say: Queen-Bee, Queen-Mom, Queen-of-Hearts, or Queen-not-yet-determined. My own crown would probably say: Queen Multi-tasker (not proud). I'd rather not multi-task, but there are days that if I want to get everything done, I have to place it on my head for a few hours.

Having days that are full of "not enough time and too much to do" is how I ended up with the "two birds with one stone" idea of a coloring/thinking kind of book. What if I can color and do some deep thinking *at the same time*? I'm always looking for ways to save time. Being a single mom, a working woman, a handy-woman at home, responsible for all things under the roof and outside of it, I don't sit quiet very often, but I still have lots of unused loose goals and old dreams laying around my house. They are hidden under the dusty end tables in the family room, buried in the bottom of the overflowing laundry basket and sit stagnant in the back of a drawer of outdated makeup. They are small, invisible puzzle-like pieces scattered everywhere, but never gathered all into one place.

After creating and coloring my own copy of this book, I now keep my dreams and goals in this one safe place, and it encourages me to grow them as I gather and spill them out onto the pages.

While I color, I'm refueling my dreams as I think about the countless ways that I want to invite them back into my life. I'm rediscovering all of the things that are most important to me and how to add more fun back into my sometimes/often-times monotonous life.

Each page is a gentle reminder or a kick in the butt, your choice. But once you start turning the pages, you'll see what I mean. Read the passage under each coloring page, and before you write your answer, color the illustration while you think about the question and how you'll answer it. As you add colors to your pictures, you'll add colors to your life. While you color, or after you've finished coloring each one, write in your answer for a better view of what you want your life to look like.

Coloring while I'm deep in thought is as close to meditation as I get. It gives me time to reflect on my life. This coloring journal encourages me to not only make the time to focus on me, but to answer many questions I don't think about often enough. Win-win.

We all love pretty, and I hope that you love your illustrations when you are finished, but what I want even more is for your life to look even prettier to you when you get to the last page; your colors and thoughts all mixed together. Your own masterpiece, because life really is art.

Have fun and may your dreams become more colorful and vibrant by the time you've finished so that they can shine even brighter than they do now.

xo Katherine

Use good quality colored pencils, or steal a stash of your child's crayons. If you really want to do it up fancy-style, watercolors are very pretty, too. The pages would need drying time, but life does too, sometimes. ☺

~Patience is a virtue~

No frustrations allowed. If you can't answer a question, it's fine. No one is going to check your answers later. You are the only one judging your work and answers, and only you can figure out what makes sense to you and your heart, soul and mind. Just don't be afraid to place those three important items down in your answers. They ARE the answers.

Have fun!

"Creativity is intelligence having fun."

~Albert Einstein

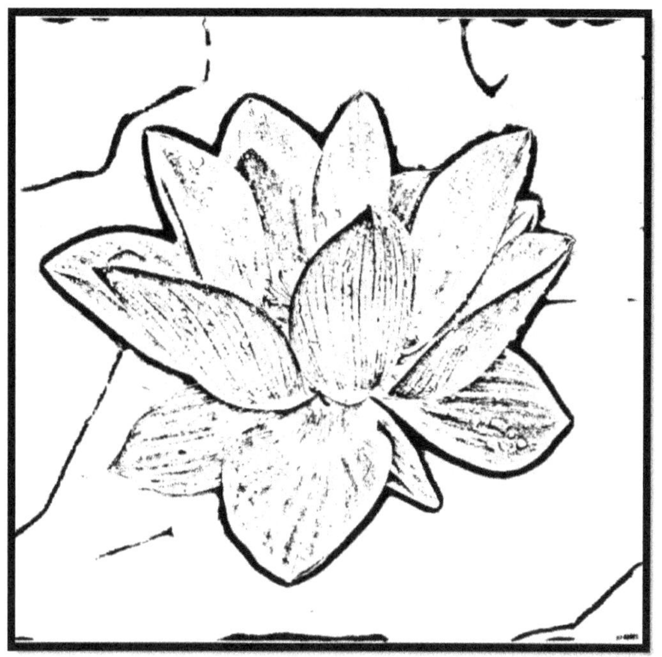

What is elegant in your life right now?

(You get to be the one to determine what "elegant" means to you and what in your life feels that way.)

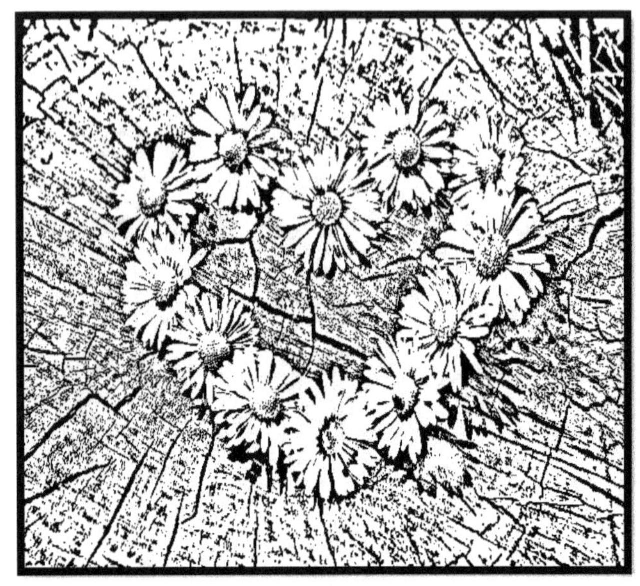

What are all the things in your life that you treasure? (Including loved ones)

____

____

____

____

____

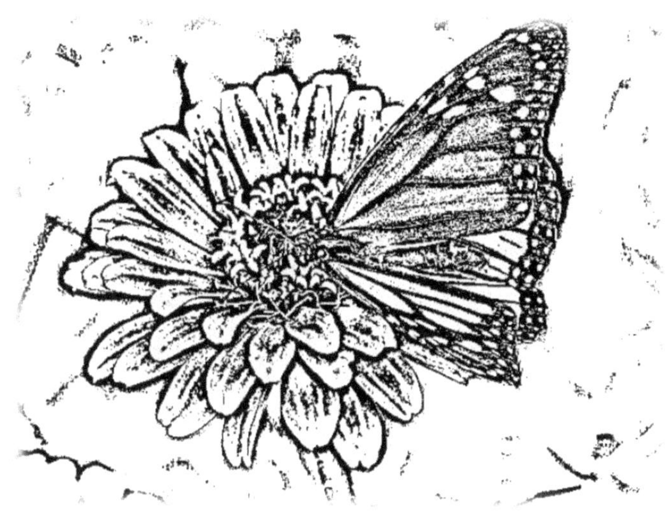

What areas in your life right now are exactly as you want them to be and bring you comfort? (Ex: What is working perfectly?)

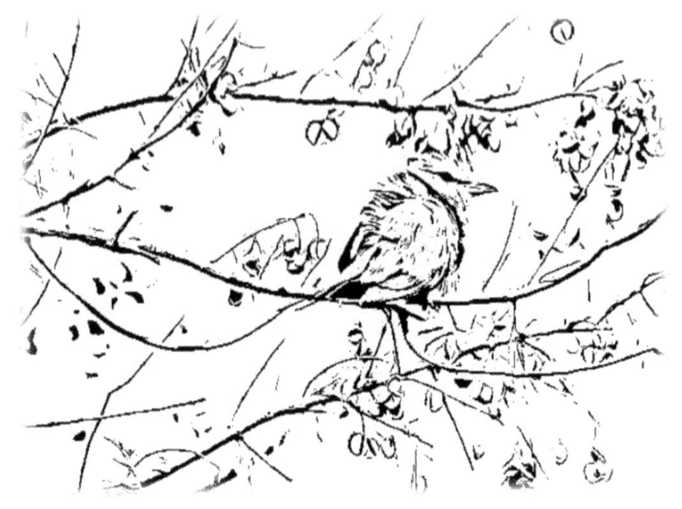

What activities and things help you to feel more peaceful?

____

____

____

____

____

____

____

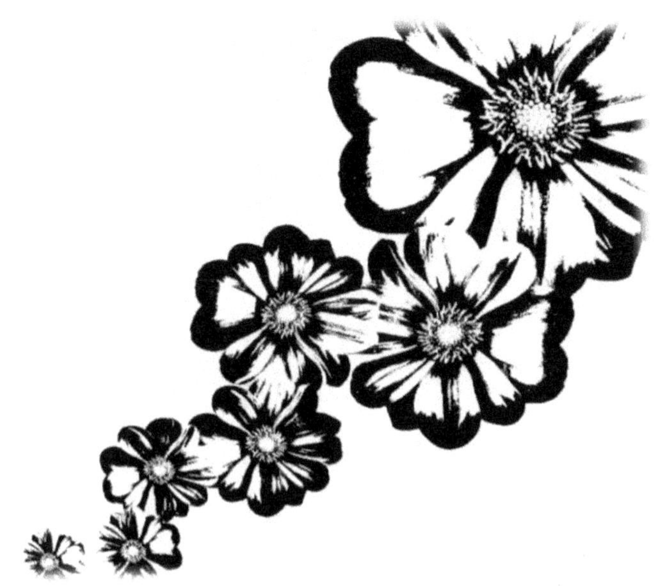

What is your dangling carrot? (What is your "calling" that you haven't reached yet?)

____

____

____

____

____

____

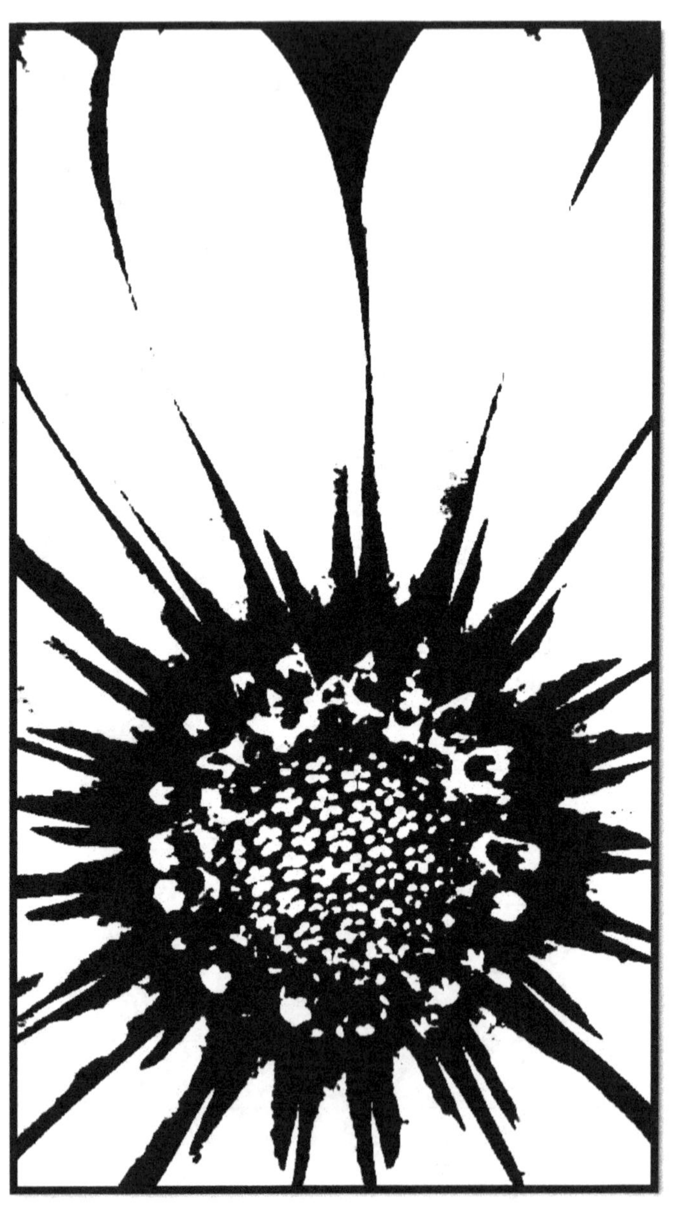

How do you take good care of yourself?

____

____

____

____

____

____

____

____

____

____

____

____

____

____

(I left a lot of spaces because I'm hoping that you have many ways of taking good care of yourself.)

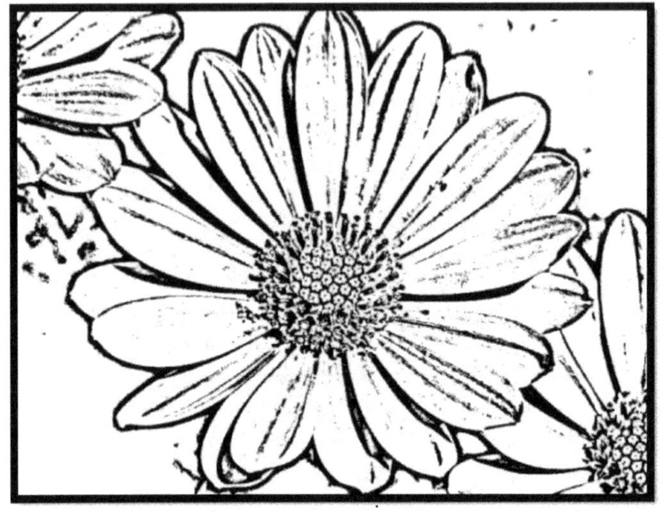

What can you do to take even better care of yourself?

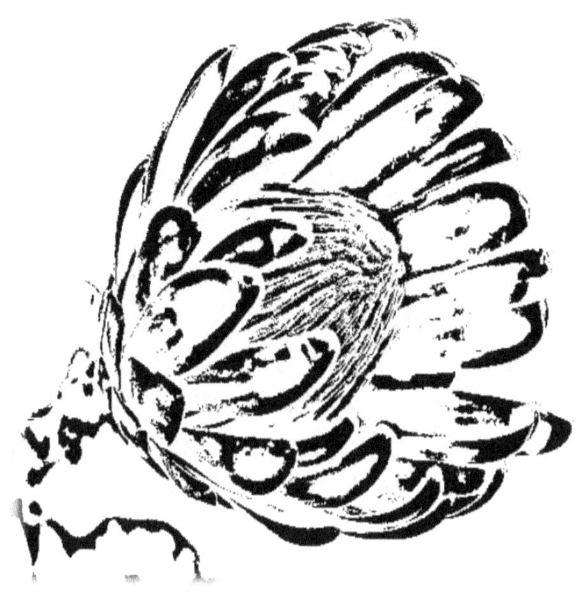

What is/are your current beasts of burden? (What is a mess or really bothers you or holds you back from enjoying life right now?)

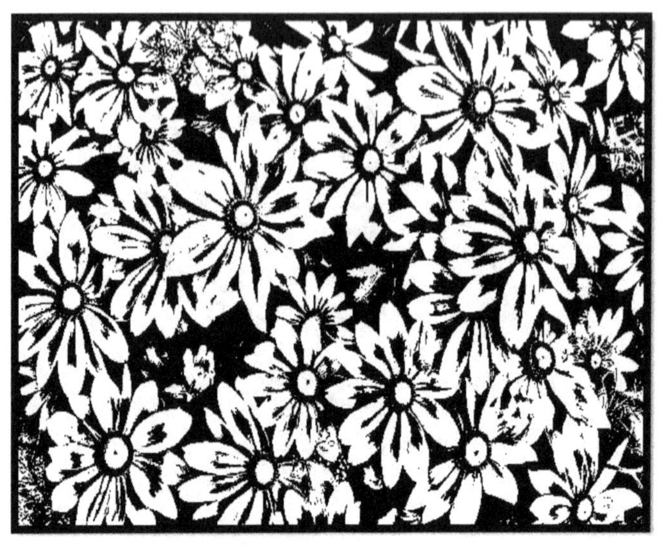

Which one/s can you fix and how?

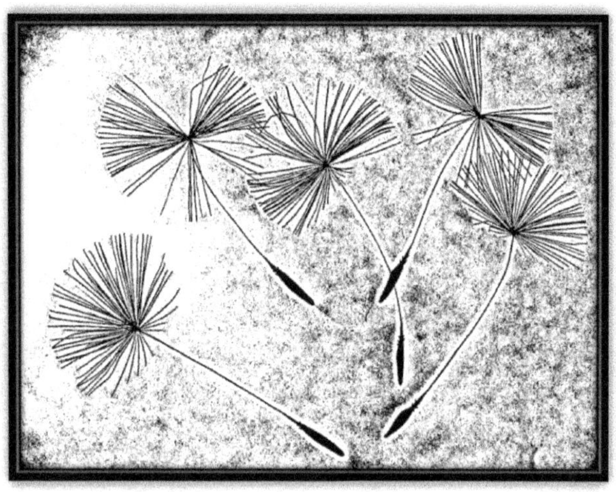

I want your life to feel special to you. In what way do you wish your life was different in order to feel more endearing and lighthearted?

____

____

____

____

____

____

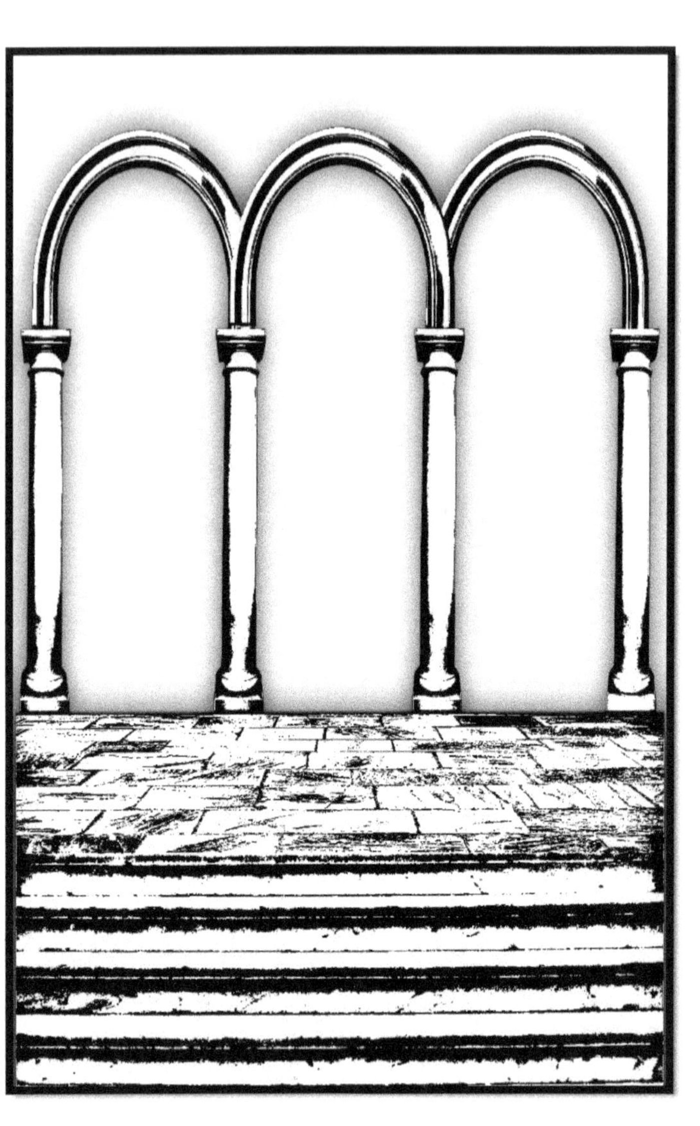

Make a list of your life-long personal growth goals that you have or want to have: (there's a place for creating a bucket list later, not here.)

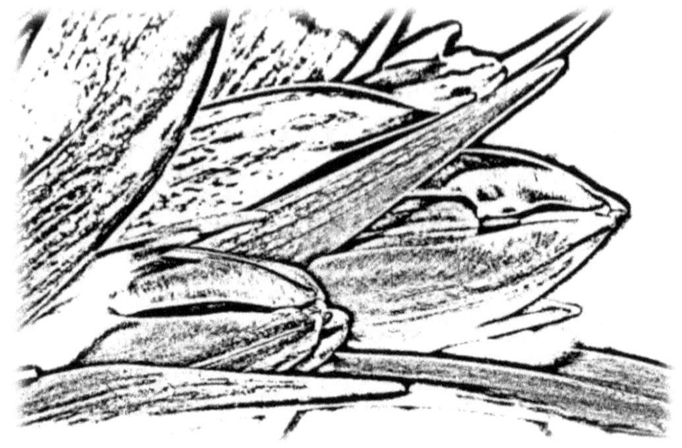

What do you want to feel at the end of each day?

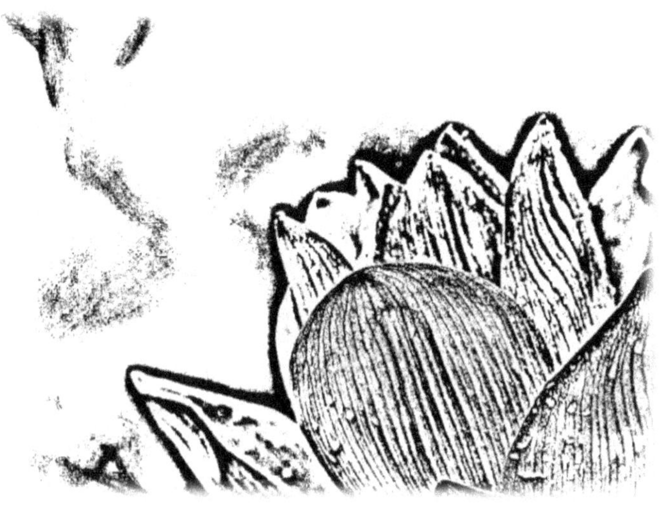

What can you do to make that happen/attainable?

____

____

____

____

____

____

____

____

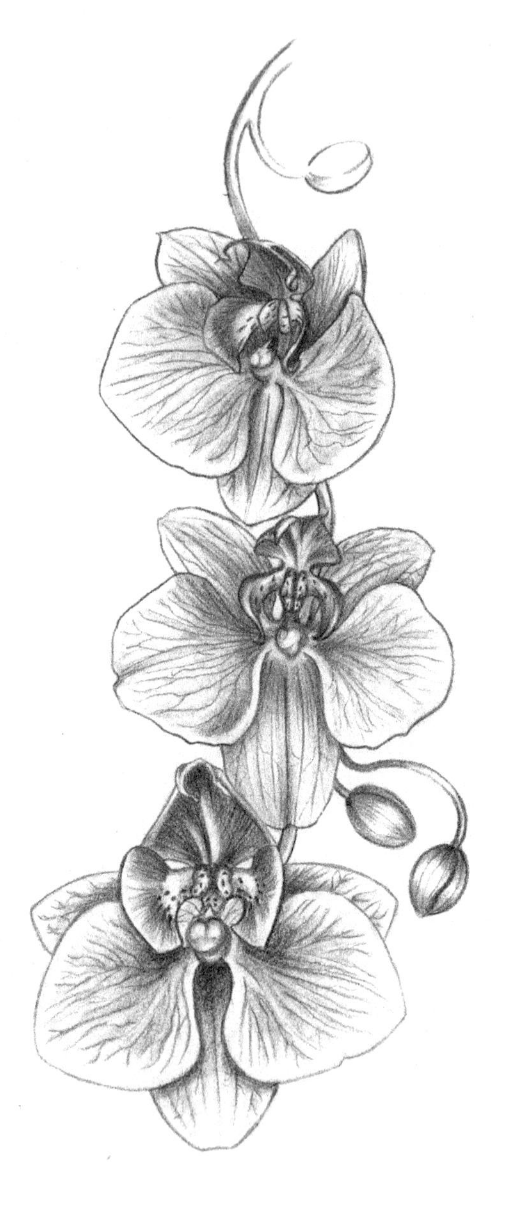

Besides family and religion, list all of your passions, whether you currently act on them or not: (this can include hobbies, career, material things, activities, arts, sports, family, etc.)

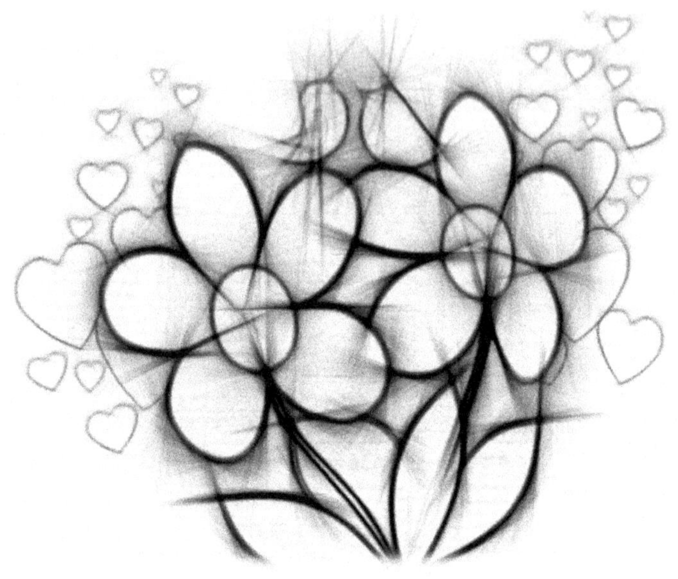

Out of all your passions, what two (2) do you want to be the most serious about?

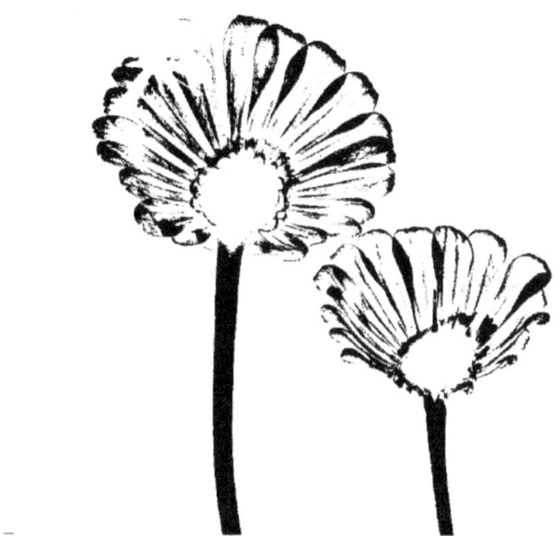

Can you do those two passions up big?

What do you need to do in order to do that?

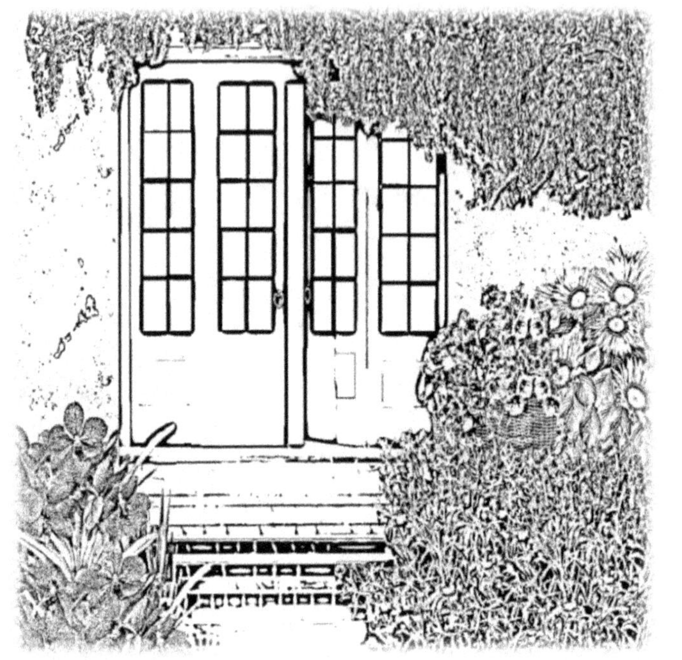

What is the biggest barrier stopping you from acting on your passions of choice?

____

____

____

____

____

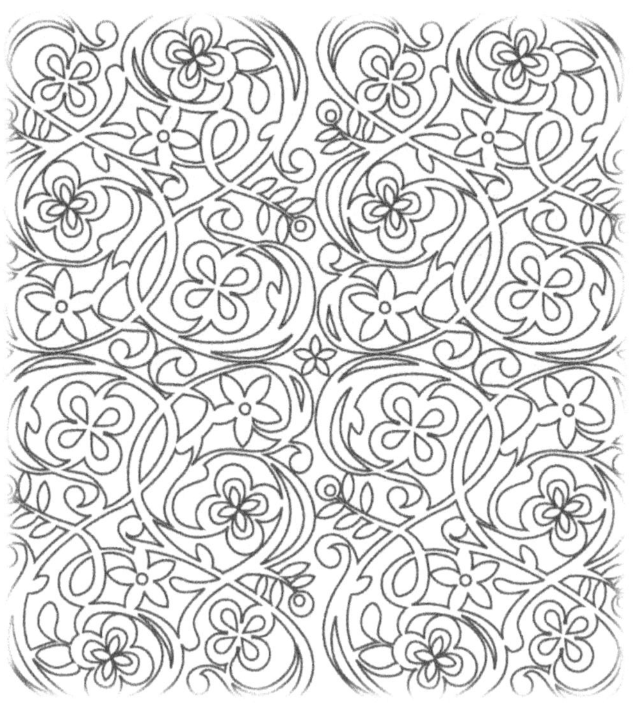

Can you remove the barriers yourself?

How can you remove them?

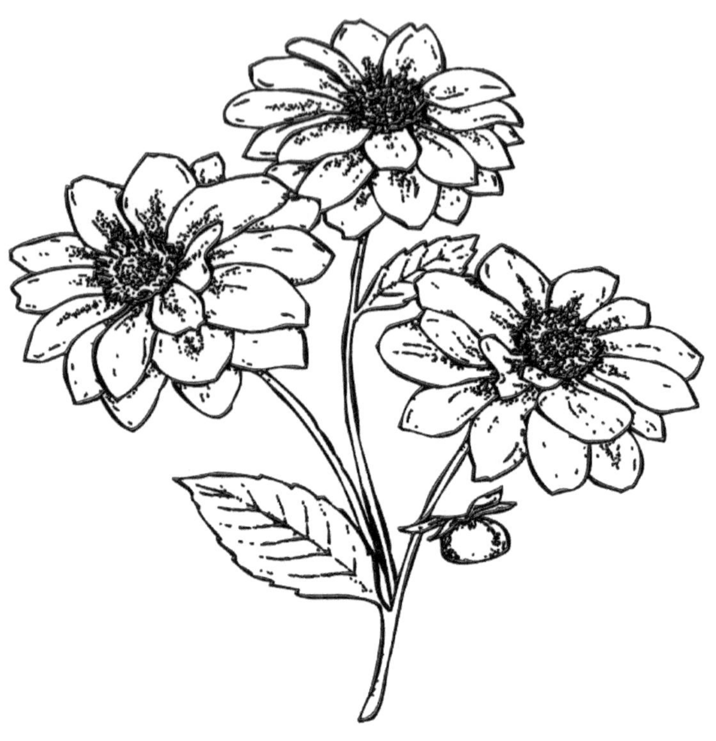

What simple activities or things make you happy?

____

____

____

____

Can you start enjoying some of them daily?

____

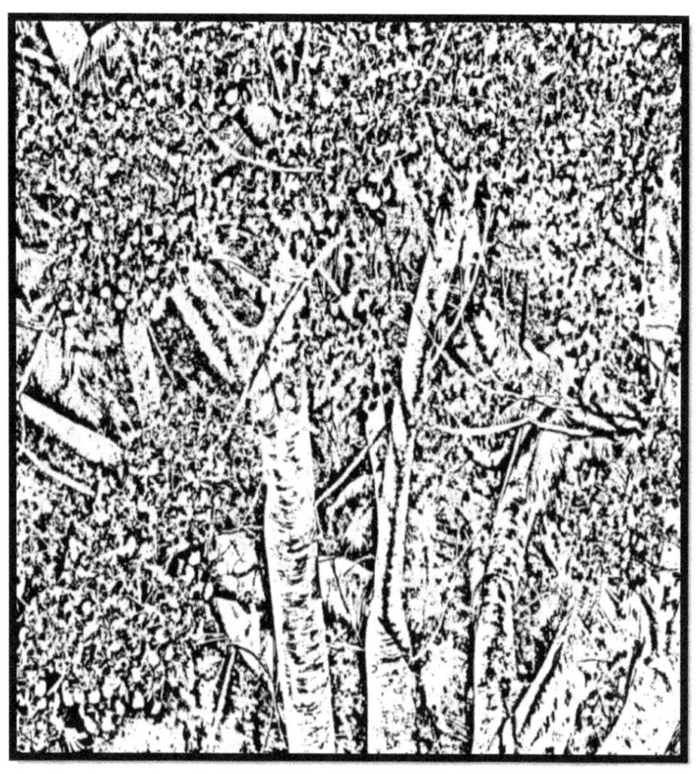

Does your smart phone and the internet interfere with the precious things in your life? _________

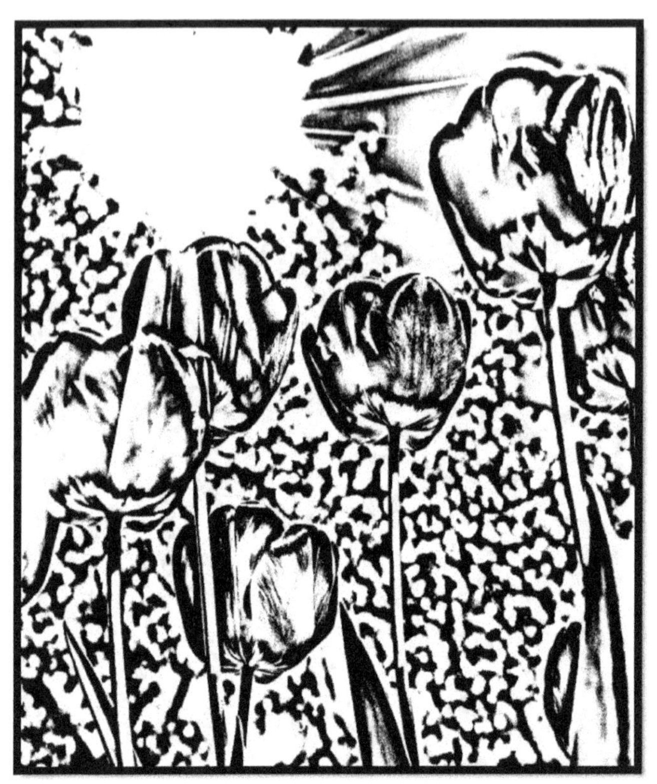

If so, how can you allow that to happen less and less?

____

____

____

____

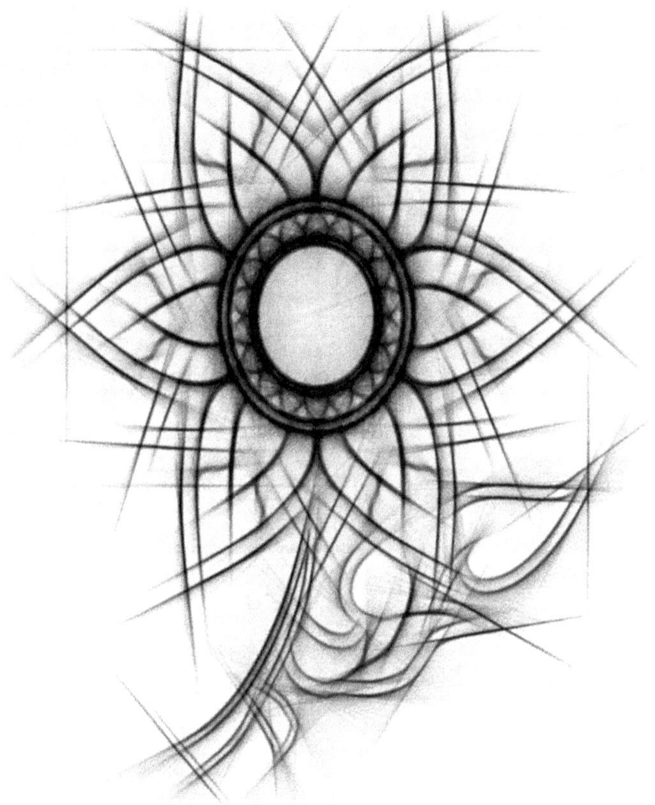

If you were to sacrifice one thing to enable you to reach your purpose/passion, what would you sacrifice?

____

____

____

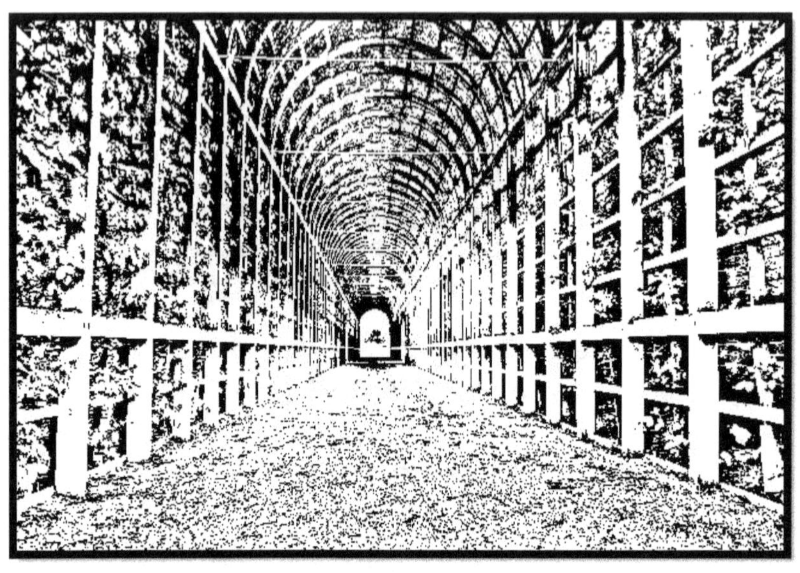

How would that sacrifice help you to reach your purpose/passion?

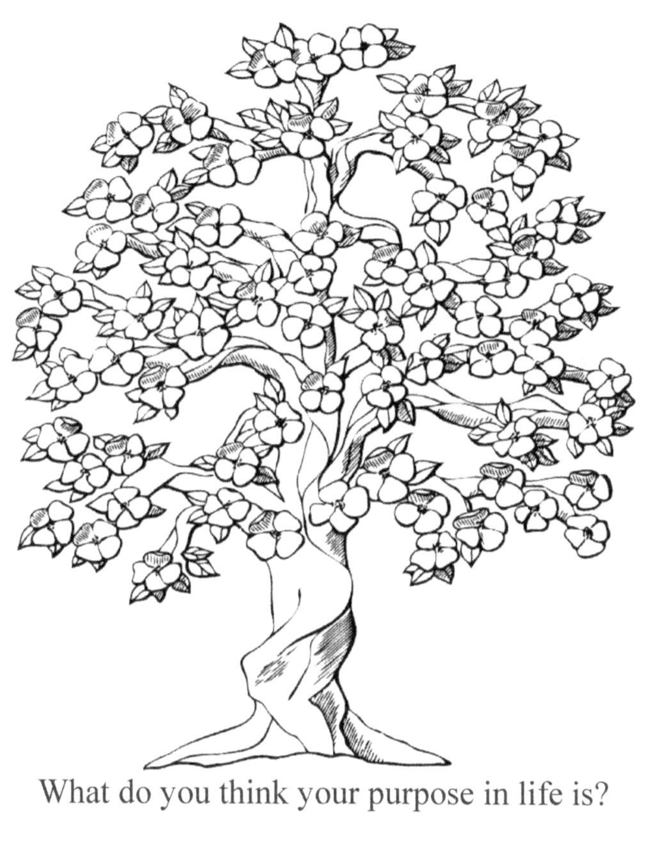

What do you think your purpose in life is?

____

____

____

____

____

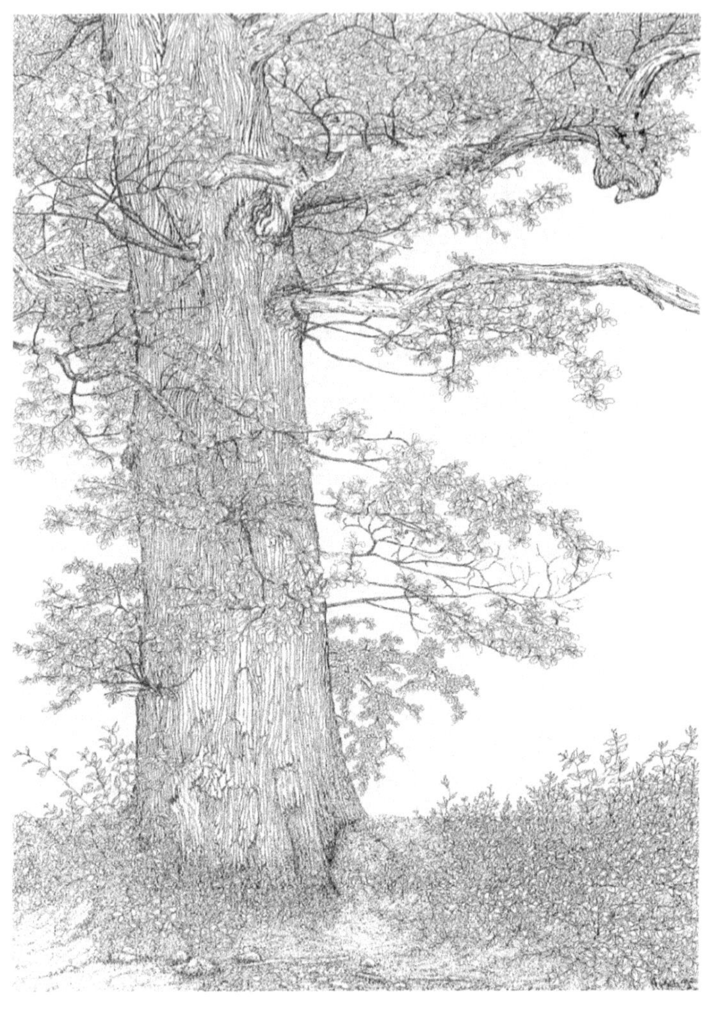

Are you living your purpose now?

____

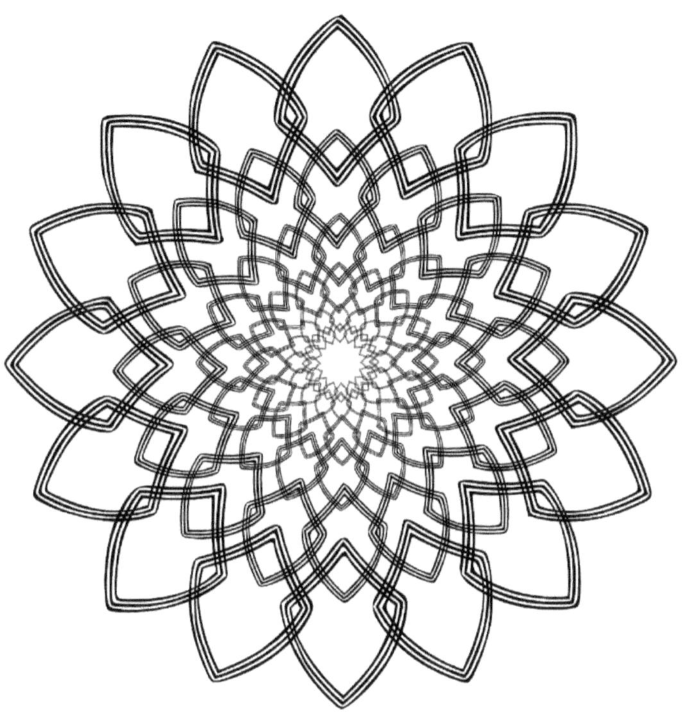

How can you be more engaged in your purpose?

____

____

____

____

____

____

What "soft landing" do you give yourself when you really need it?

(You need one in order to thrive, so make sure that you come up with a few.)

____

____

____

____

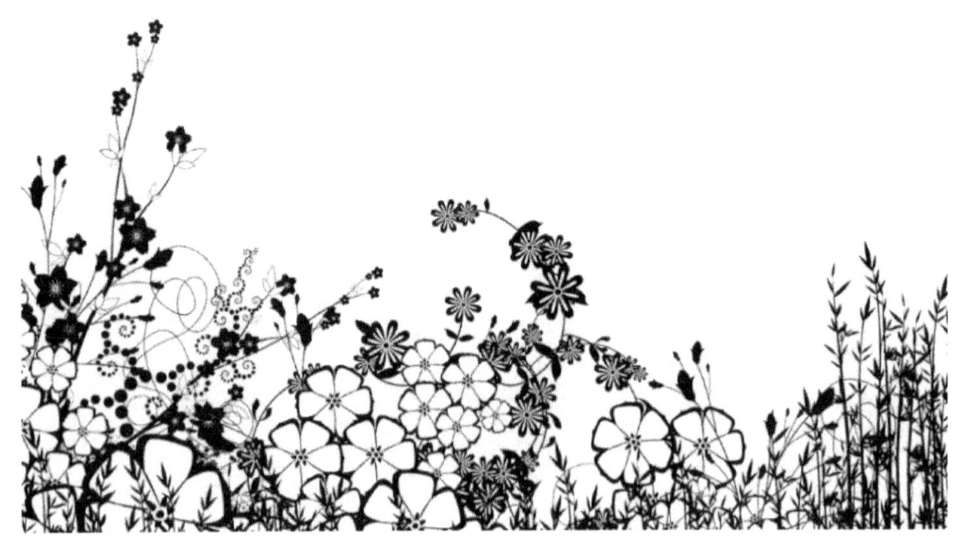

How can you do those things more often?

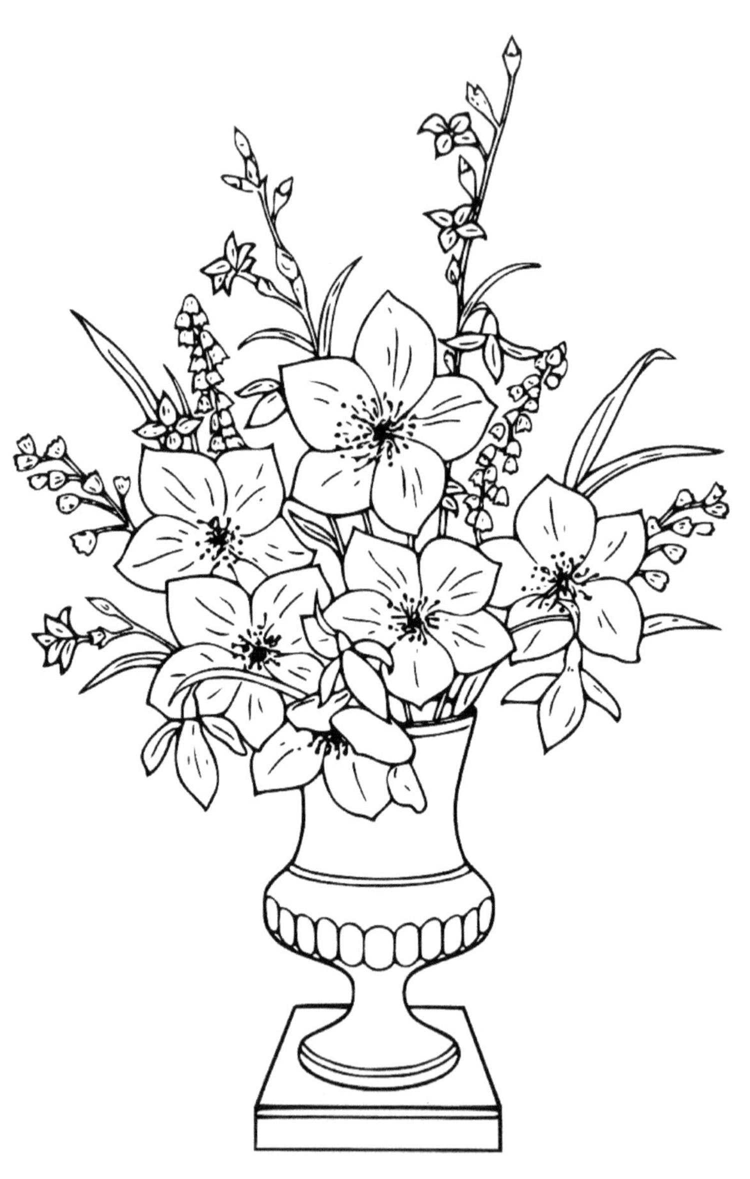

What is your favorite day of the week?

____

How do you celebrate it?

How can you celebrate it even better?

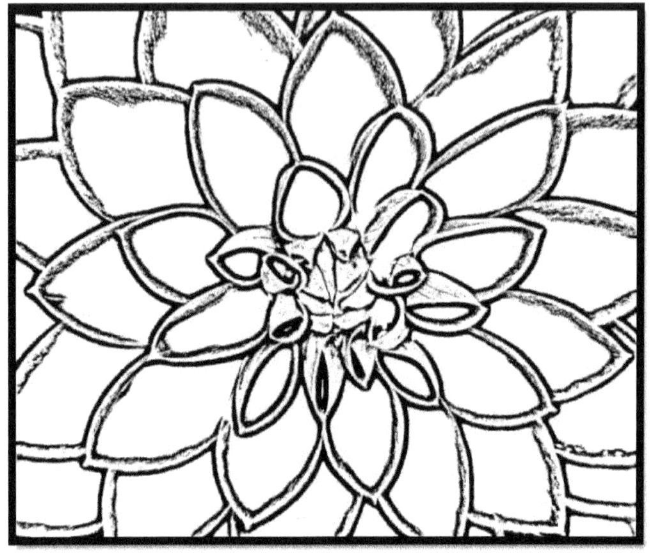

What is your favorite book?

____

If you don't know, make it a goal to know by the end of the year.

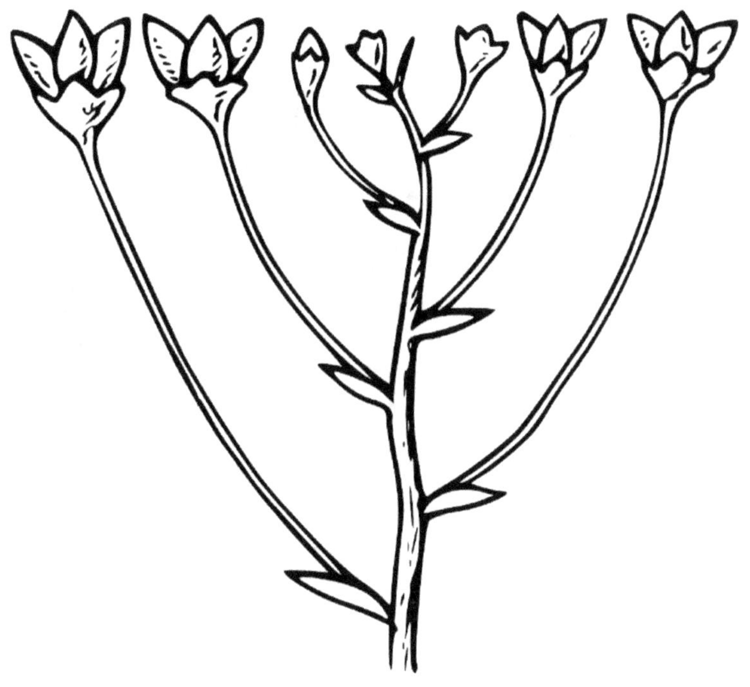

Who is your favorite author?

____

If you don't know, make it a goal to know by the end of the year.

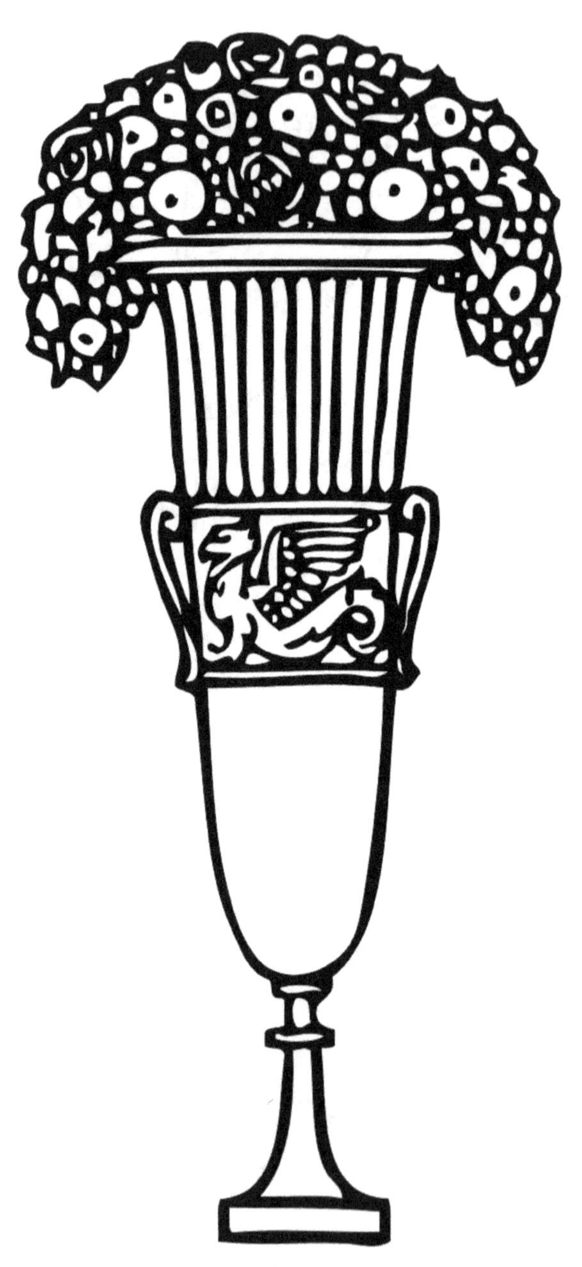

What is your favorite poem?

If you don't have one, be on a hunt for one and come back and write it here, or write your own.

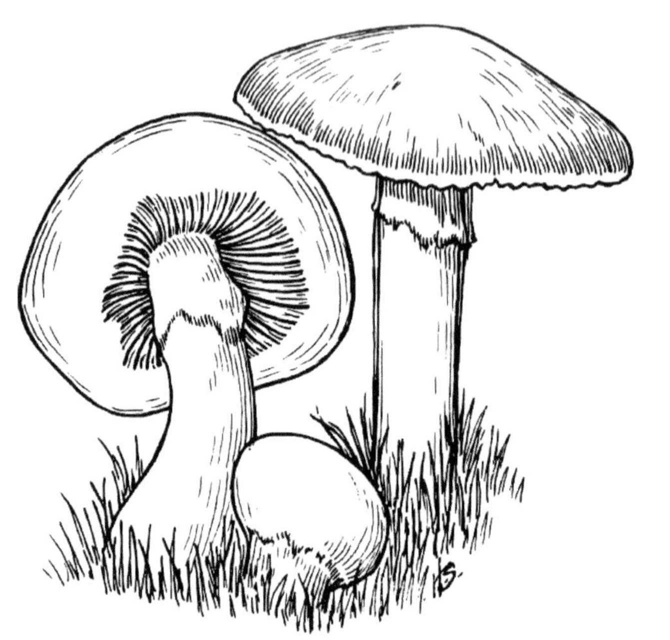

What do you like to do on a stormy day?

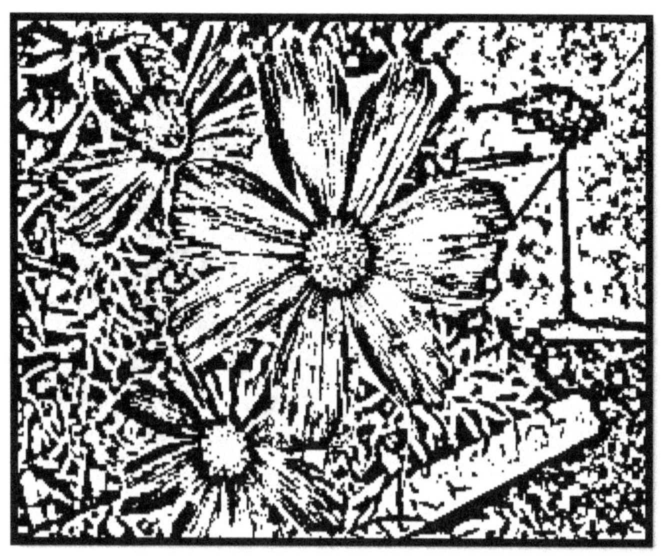

What things remind you of and bring you back to your happy childhood days?

____

____

____

____

____

____

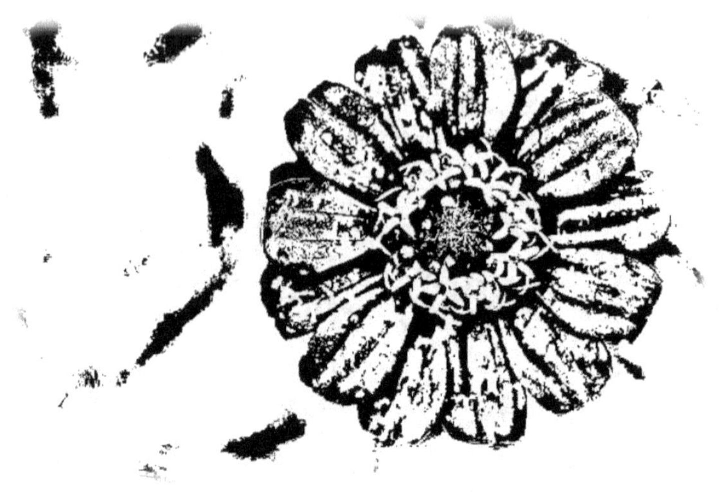

What is your go-to comfort food?
Describe it in detail.

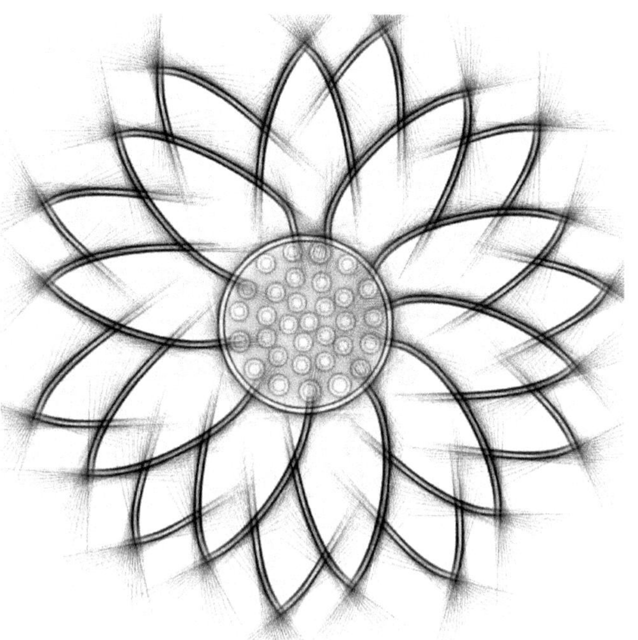

Where do you like to go when you want a quiet place? Describe it.

____

____

____

____

____

____

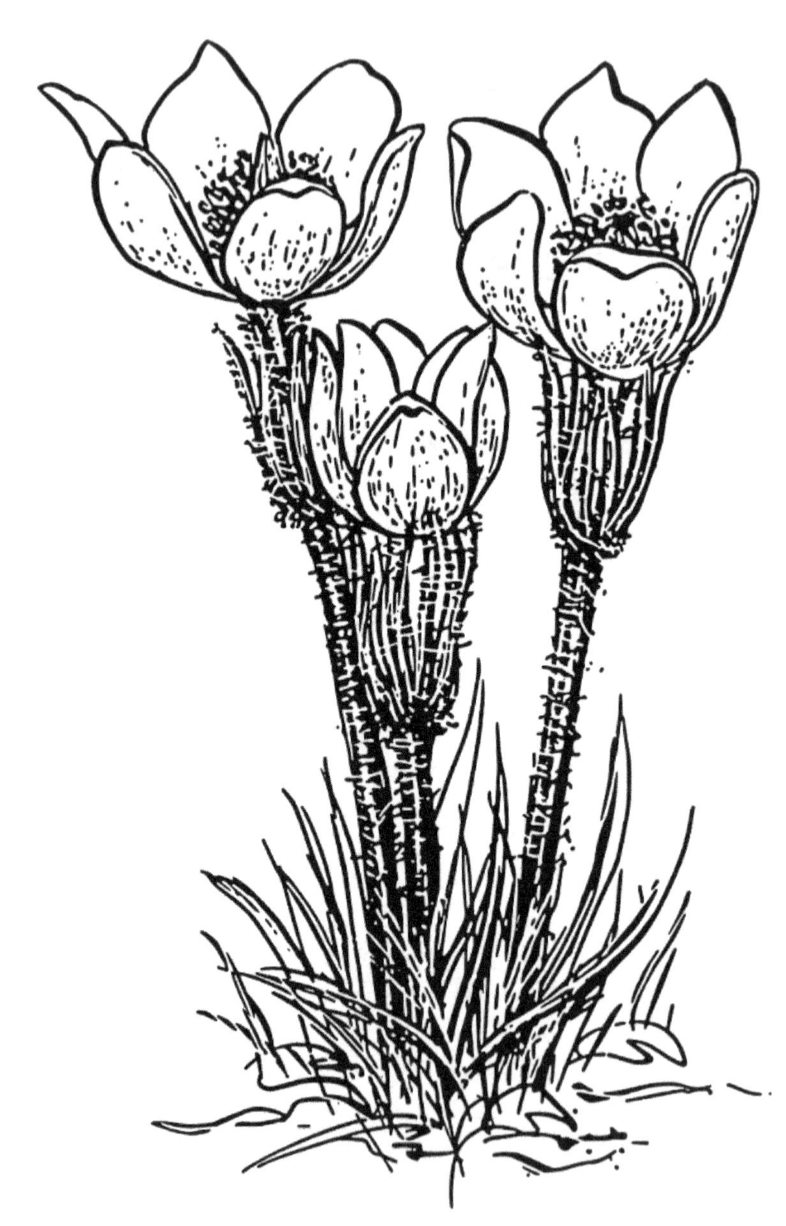

Now create a bucket list for yourself, that's not a personal growth bucket list, but a fun, exciting, challenging, simple, easy, interesting list of goals that are do-able for you.

____

____

____

____

____

____

____

____

____

____

____

____

If you need help with this one, I have a free printable on my website to help you create your bucket list: www.backtobeingawoman.com

Under "Free Printables"

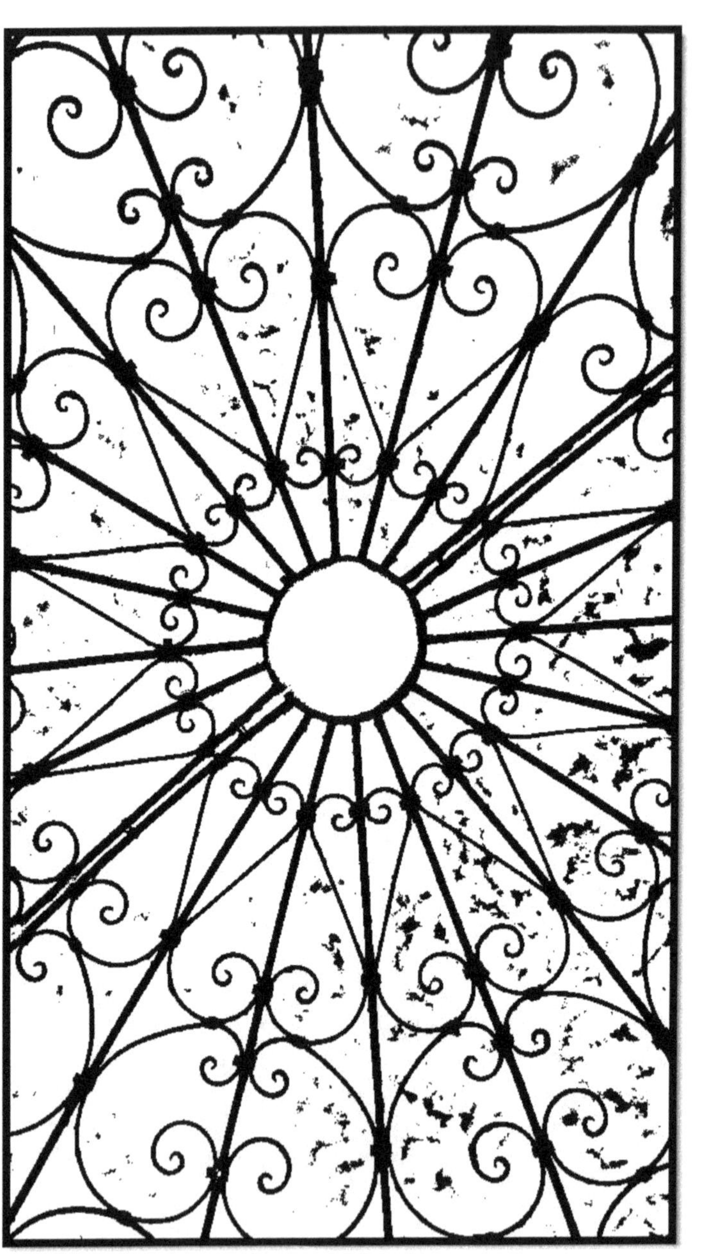

Last 2 questions. What is your definition of happy?

____

____

____

____

Are you happy? ________

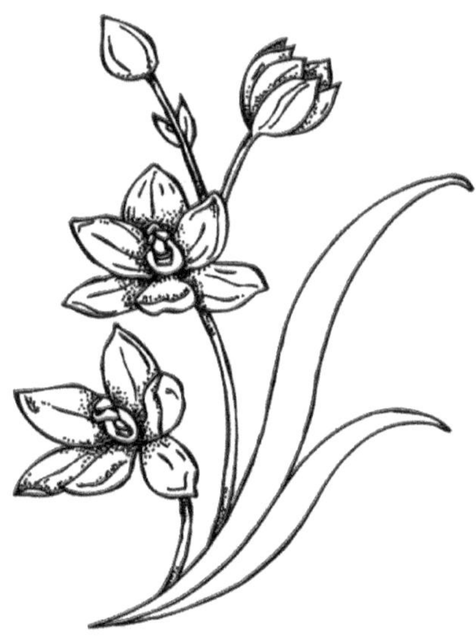

If your answer is "no," these questions are intended to bring you closer to it.

If your answer is "yes," I hope you will continue to keep happiness as the main focus in your life.

"Do not dwell in the past, do not dream of the future, concentrate the mind on the present moment."

~Buddha

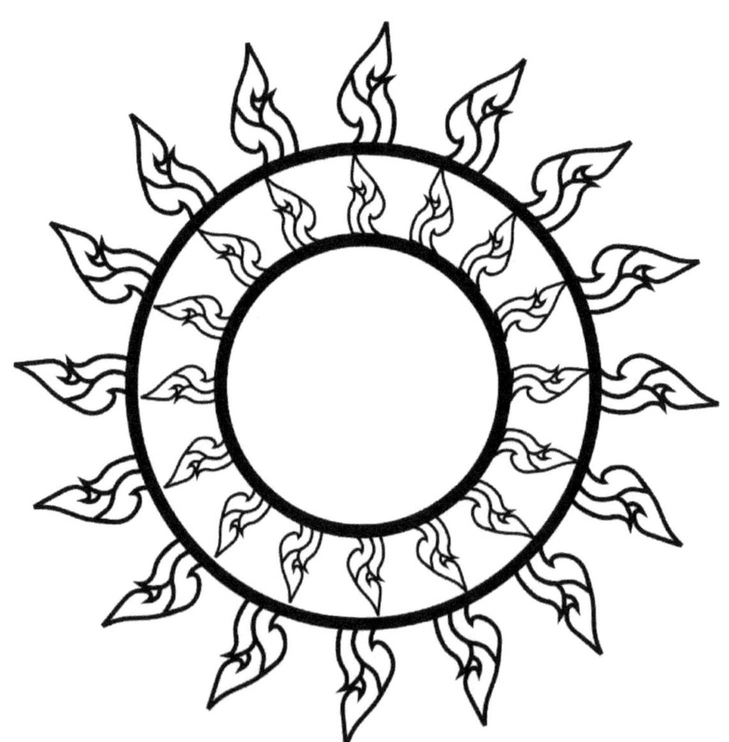

You've finished your masterpiece! Don't worry if you weren't able to answer all of the questions or even if you've colored outside of the lines. Within 66 pages, you've thought about some of the most important questions about your life and invoked some really good answers. I've asked those questions in order to get you thinking more about the masterpiece that you are living. You are bright enough to know the answers better than anyone. I didn't answer all of my questions, but now they will float around in my head and I will keep my eyes open for the answers when they show up. Being more aware of my life will help me to enjoy it more, and that's what I want for you.

I hope you've created beautiful pages and realized new discoveries about who you are, about your beliefs, dreams and your passions.

If you have dreams, you have seeds that are waiting to grow. I've given you some fertilizer, sun and water to nourish them.

This is the start of your intricate garden. Don't let the ideas and the answers end here. Come back often and visit your pages to remind yourself and to renew yourself. There's a lot of evidence you've written down to illuminate who you are and who you want to be.

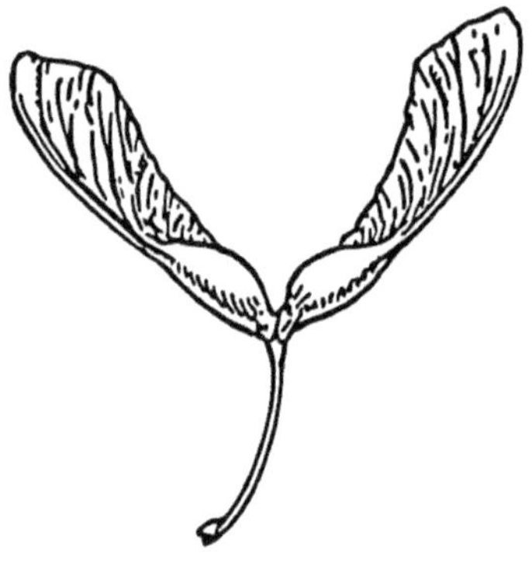

You Grow, Girl!

~A Bouquet for You~

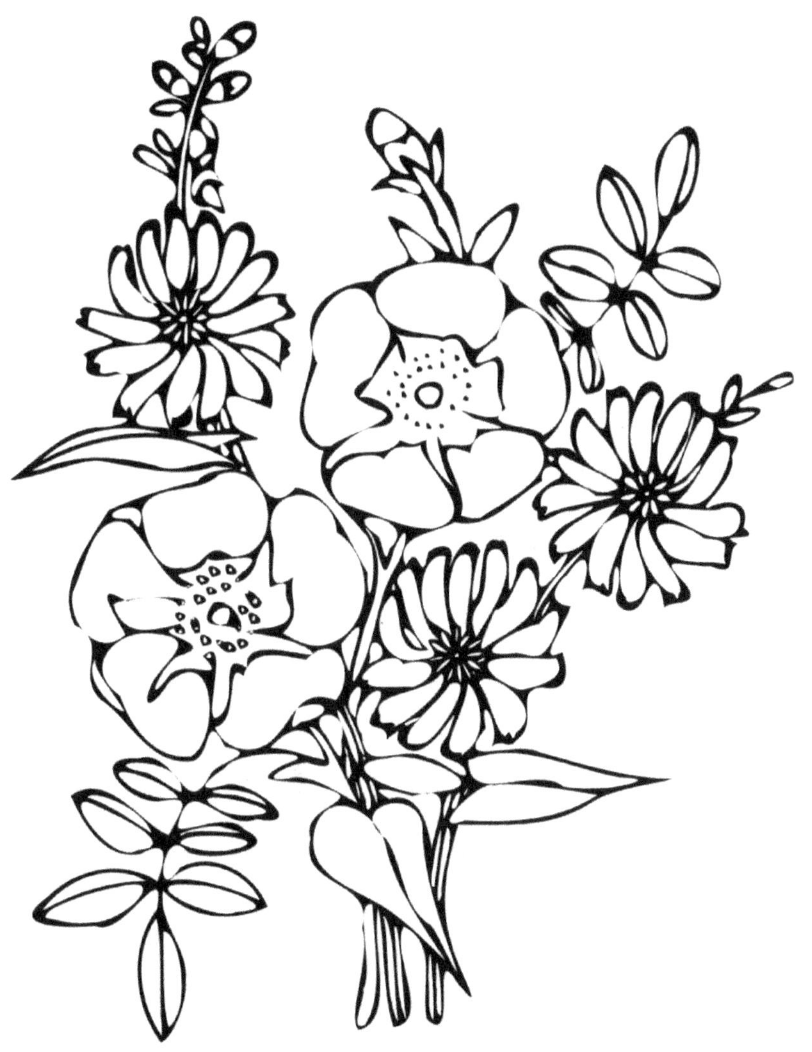

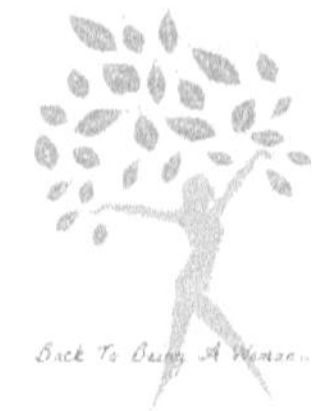

Katherine A. Rayne lives in South Florida and loves being a mom of two perfections, loves the beach, writing, sketching, reading and blogging. She is a preschool teacher, author and blogger as well as a happy mom.

She founded the community

www.BackToBeingAWoman.com

to support busy women in their life journey.

"We are all in this together."

∞

Find Katherine at:

www.Facebook.com/BackToBeingAWoman

www.Instagram.com/BackToBeingAWoman

www.Twitter.com/BeingAWoman

www.BackToBeingAWoman.com

www.Amazon.com/KatherineARayne

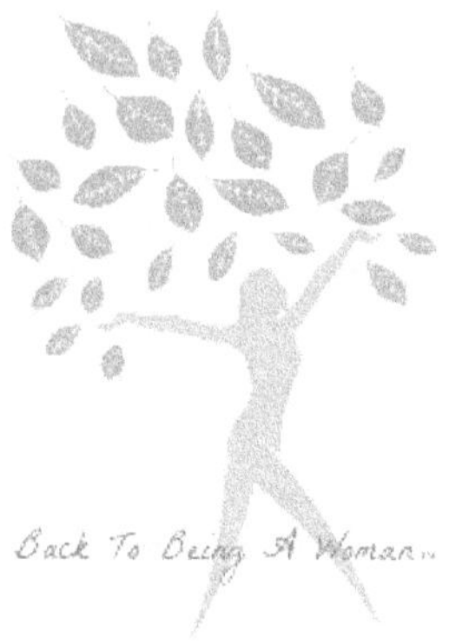

Notes

Notes

www.ingramcontent.com/pod-product-compliance
Lightning Source LLC
LaVergne TN
LVHW010943110826
845149LV00013B/2732